SNOOPY

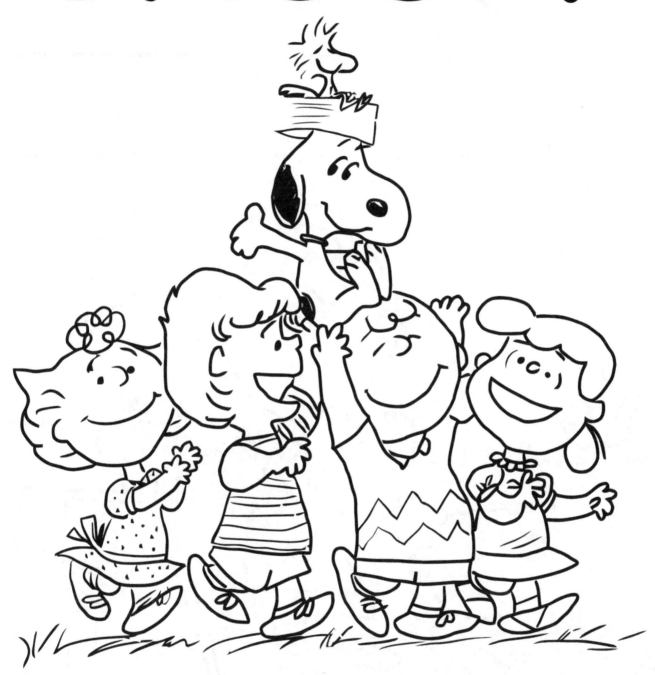

COLORING BOOK

COPYRIGHT © 2020 - ALL RIGHTS RESERVED.

THIS BOOK BELONGS TO

_____

_____

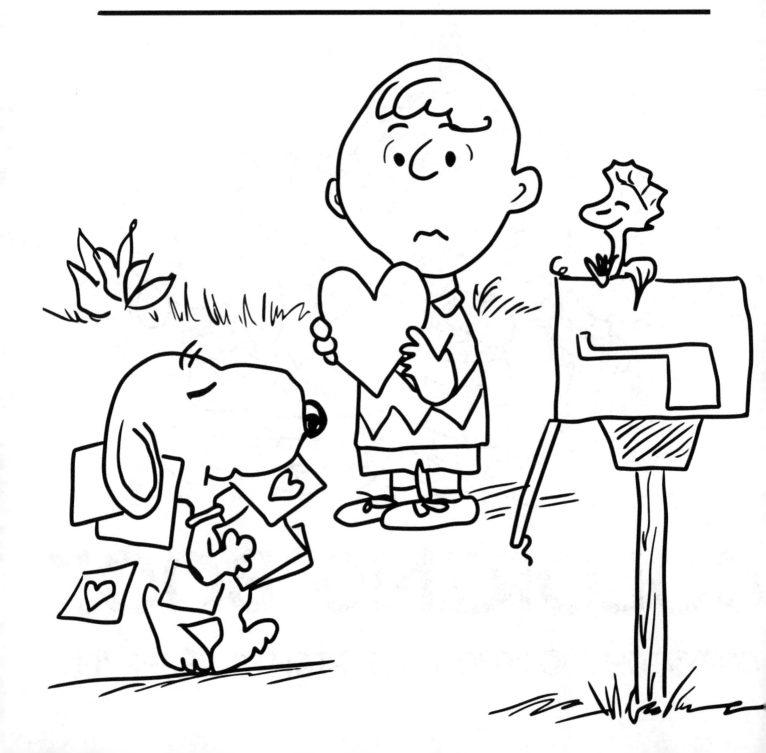

COLOR TEST PAGE

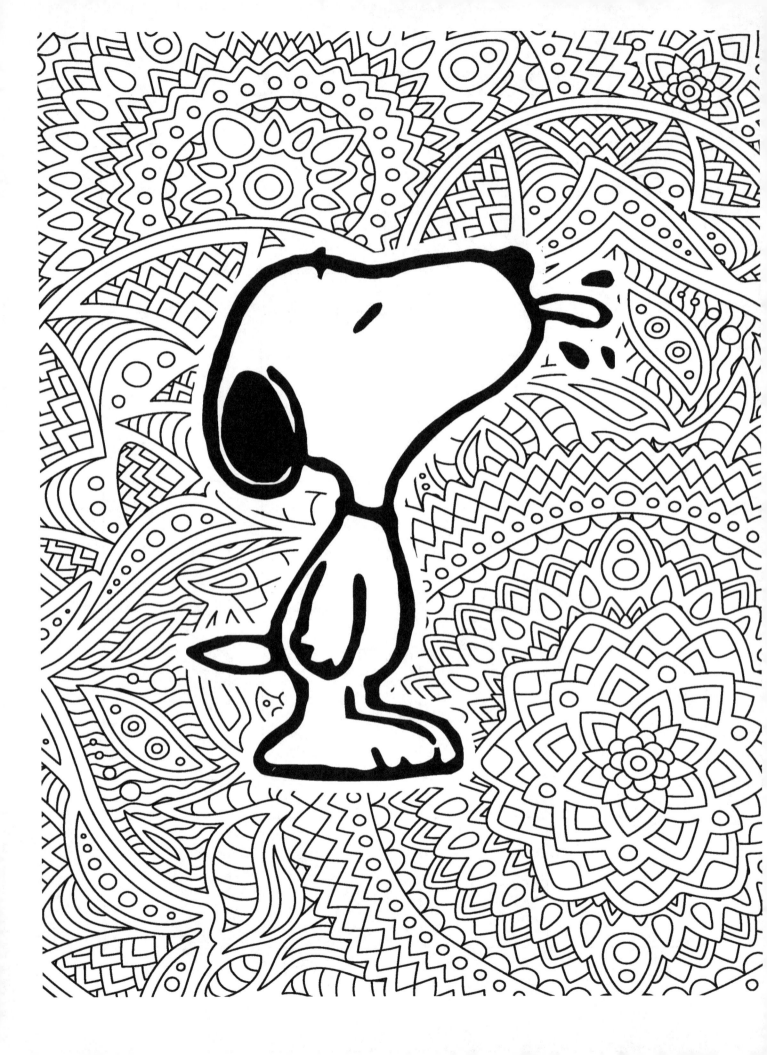

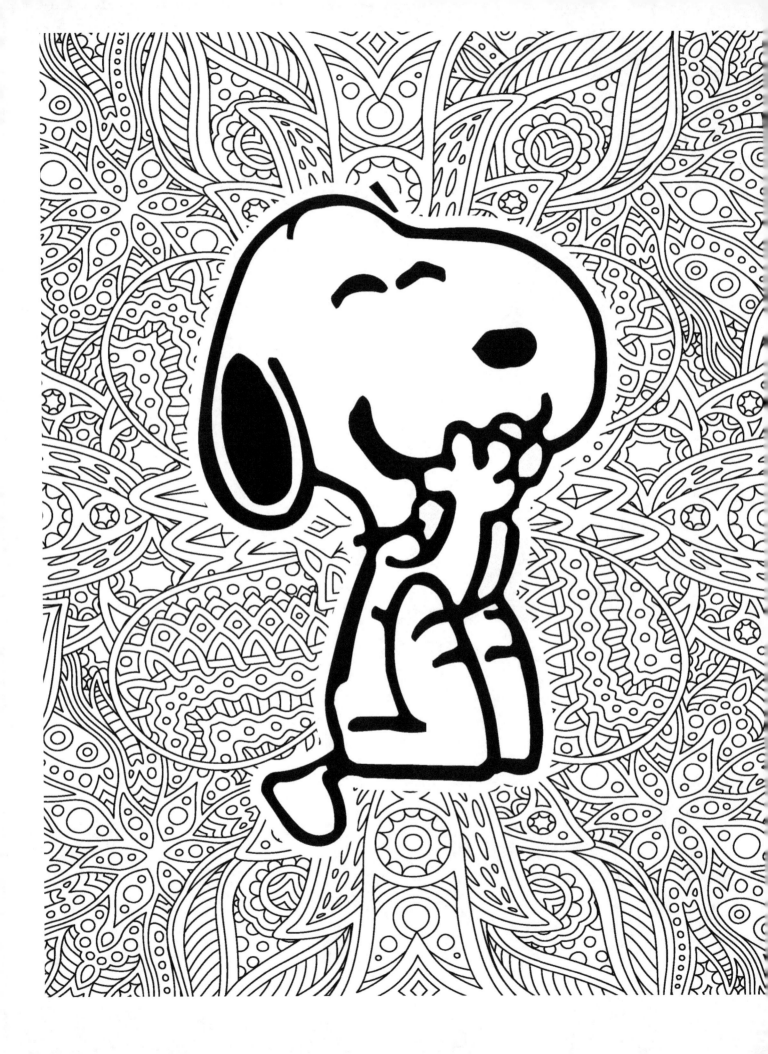

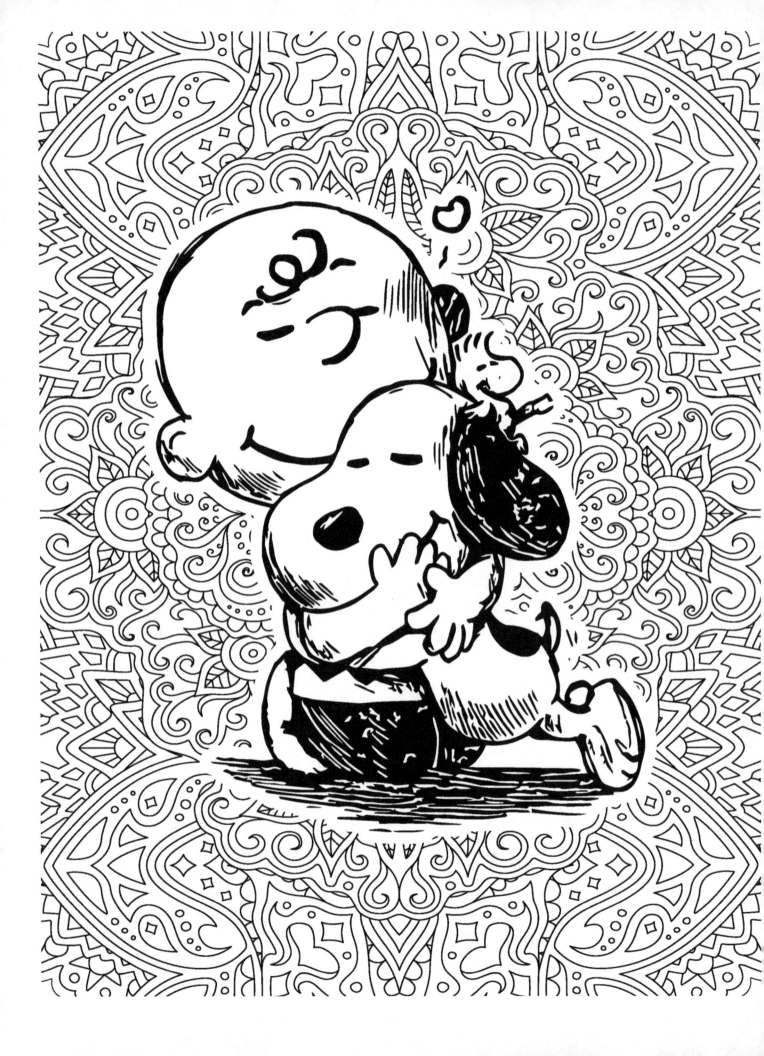

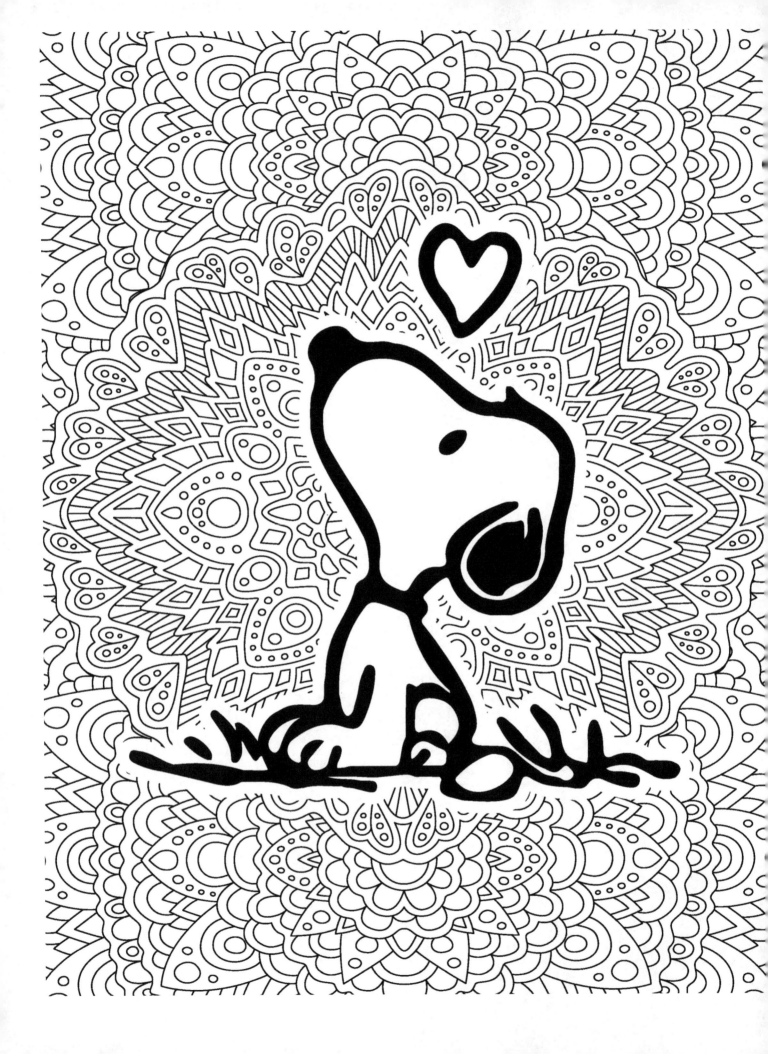

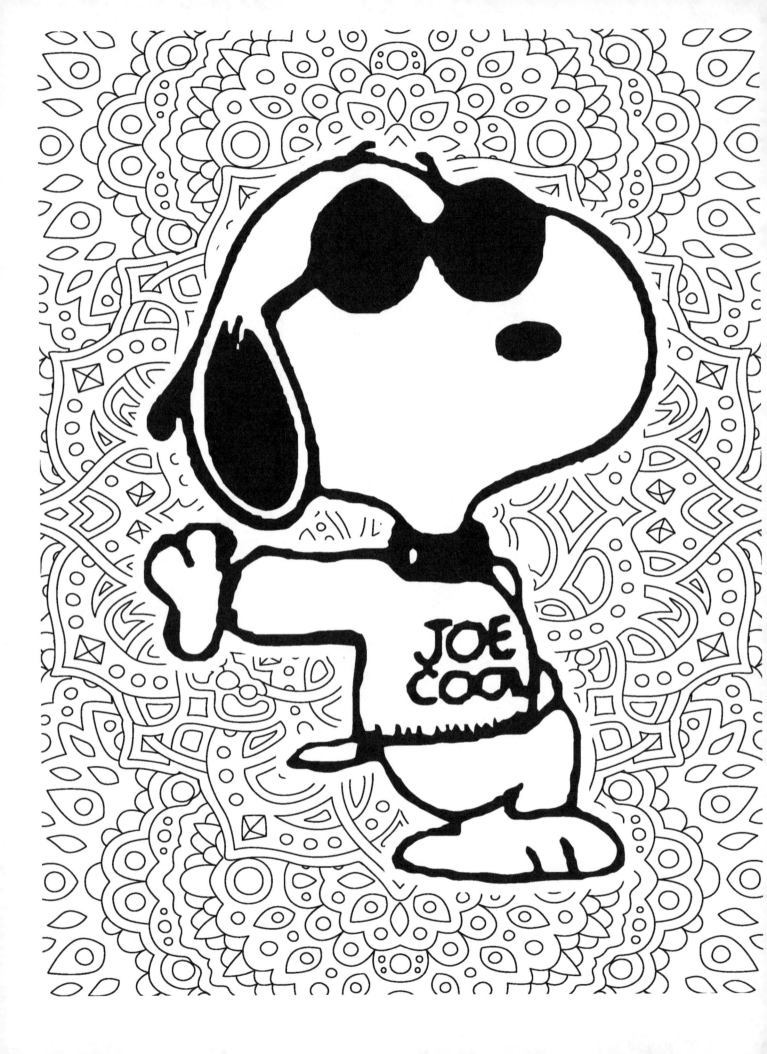

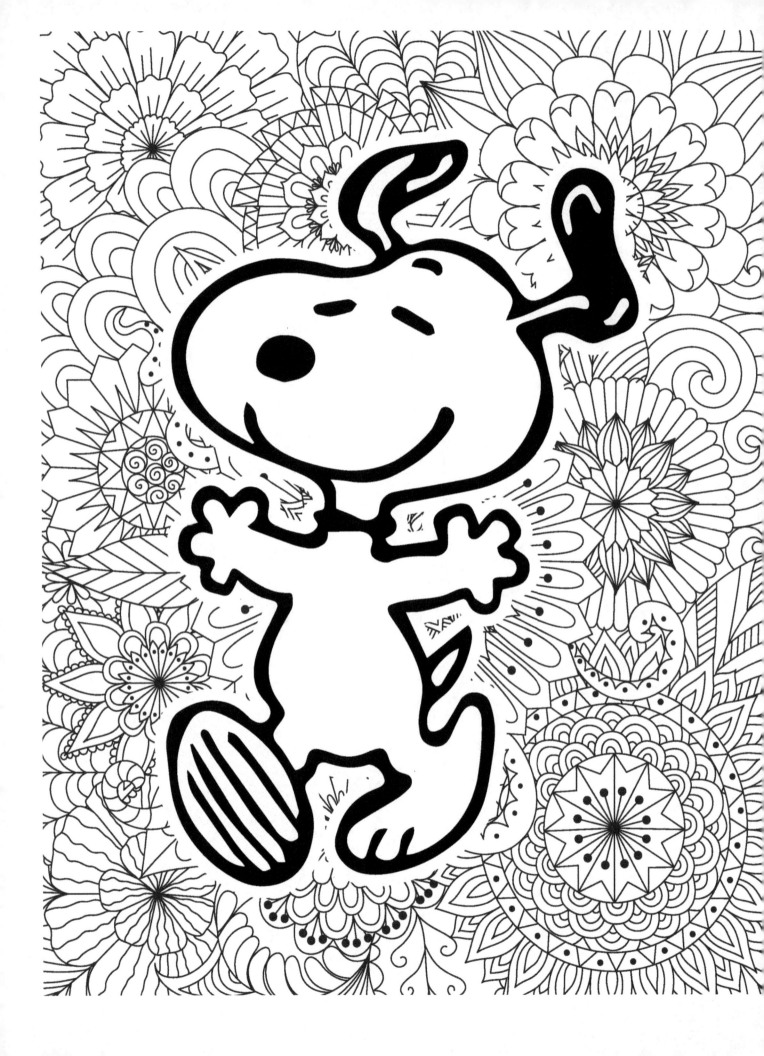

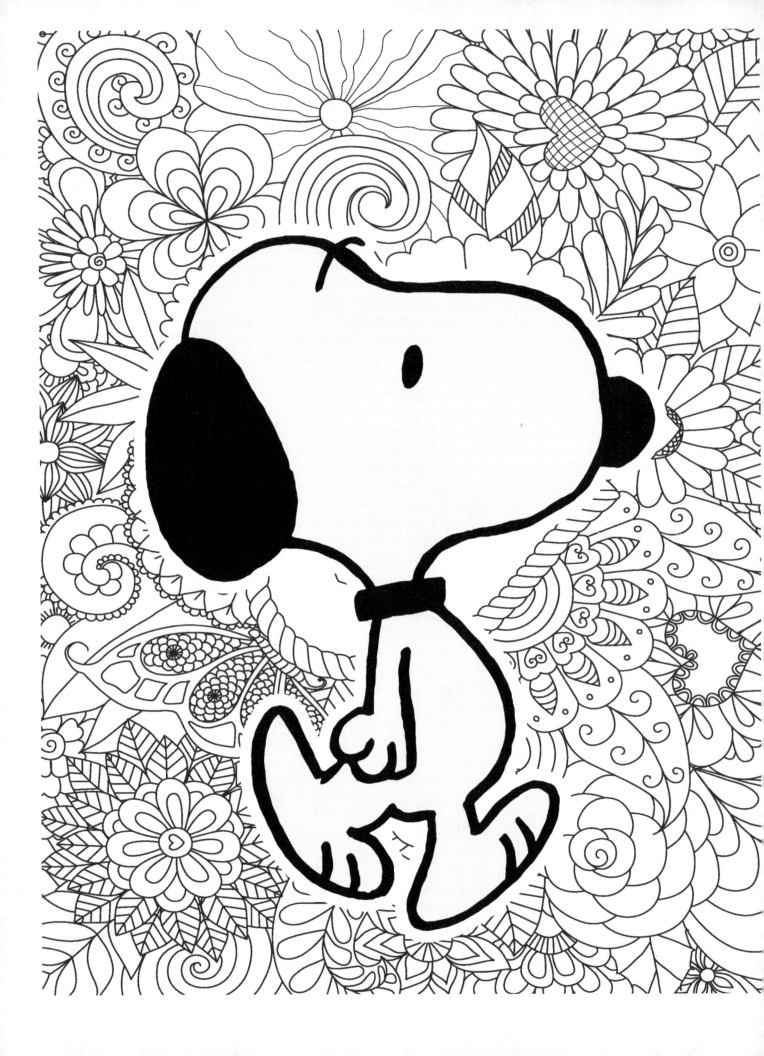

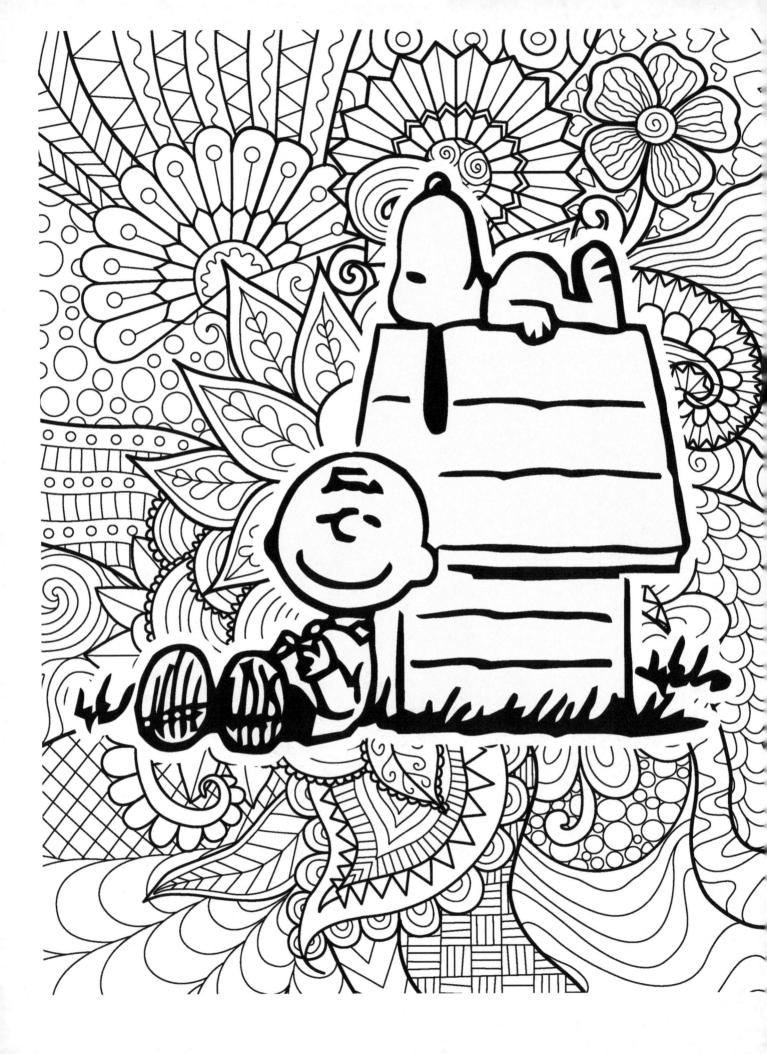

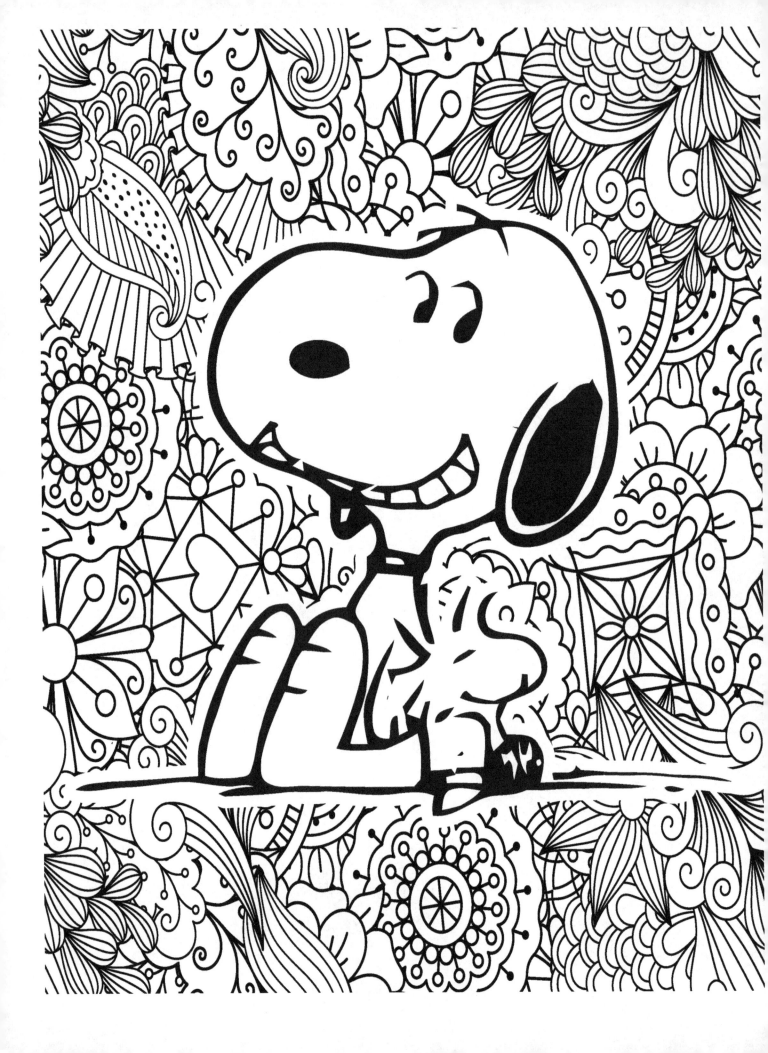

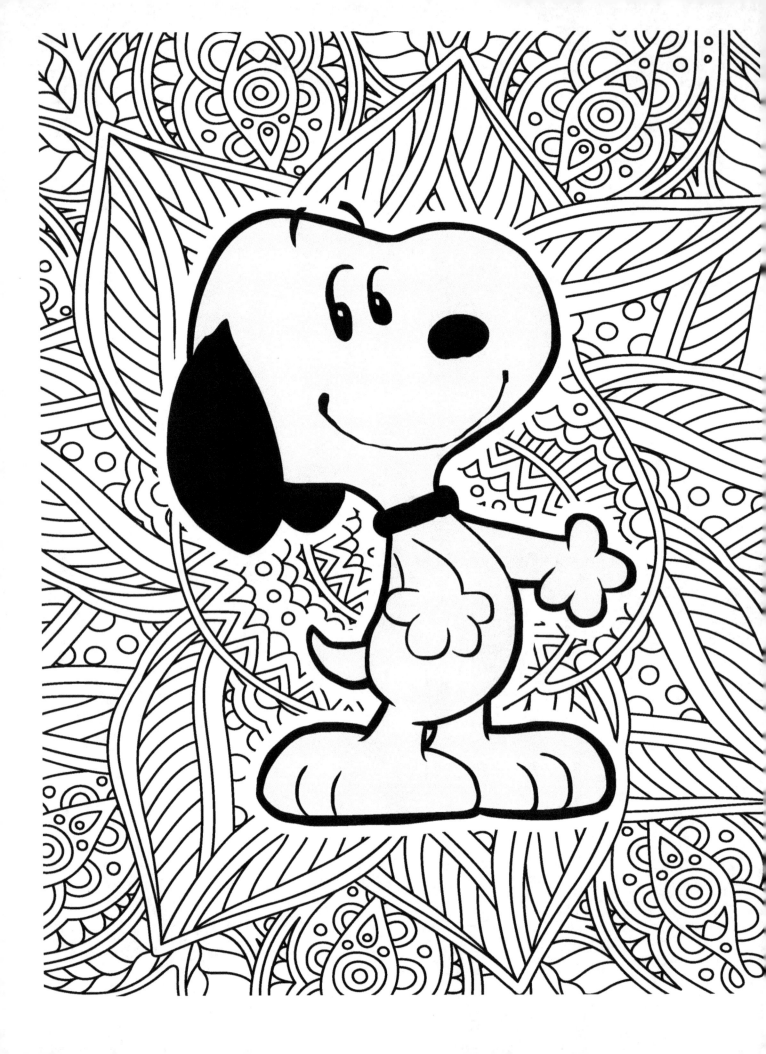

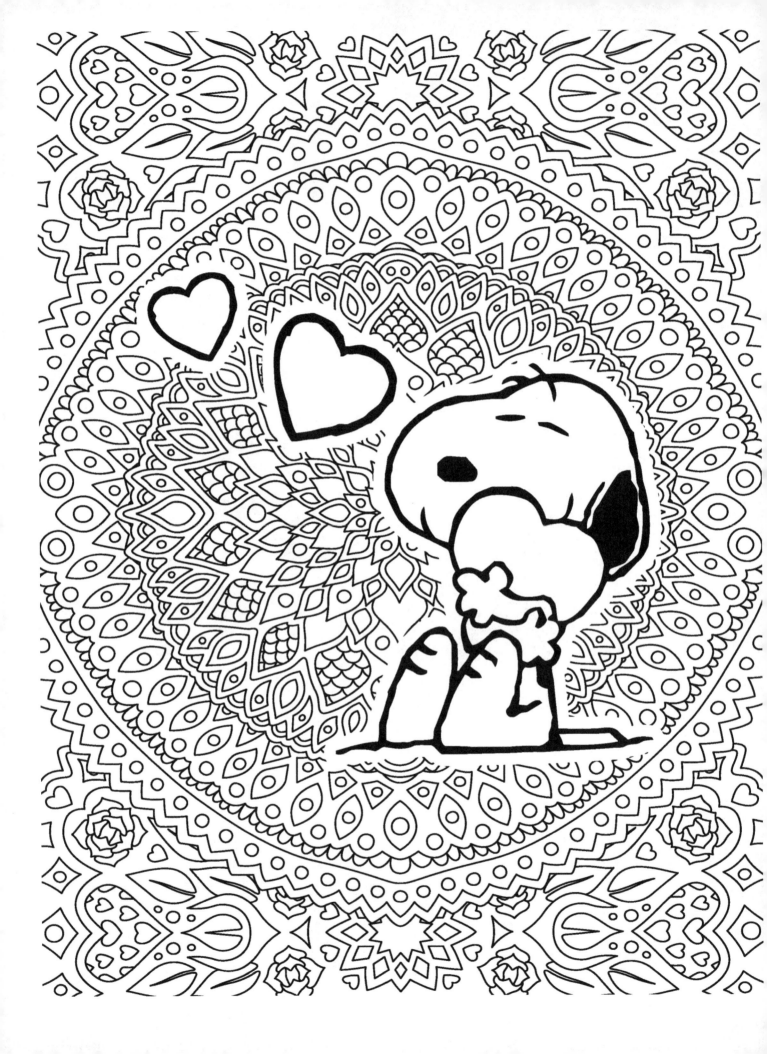

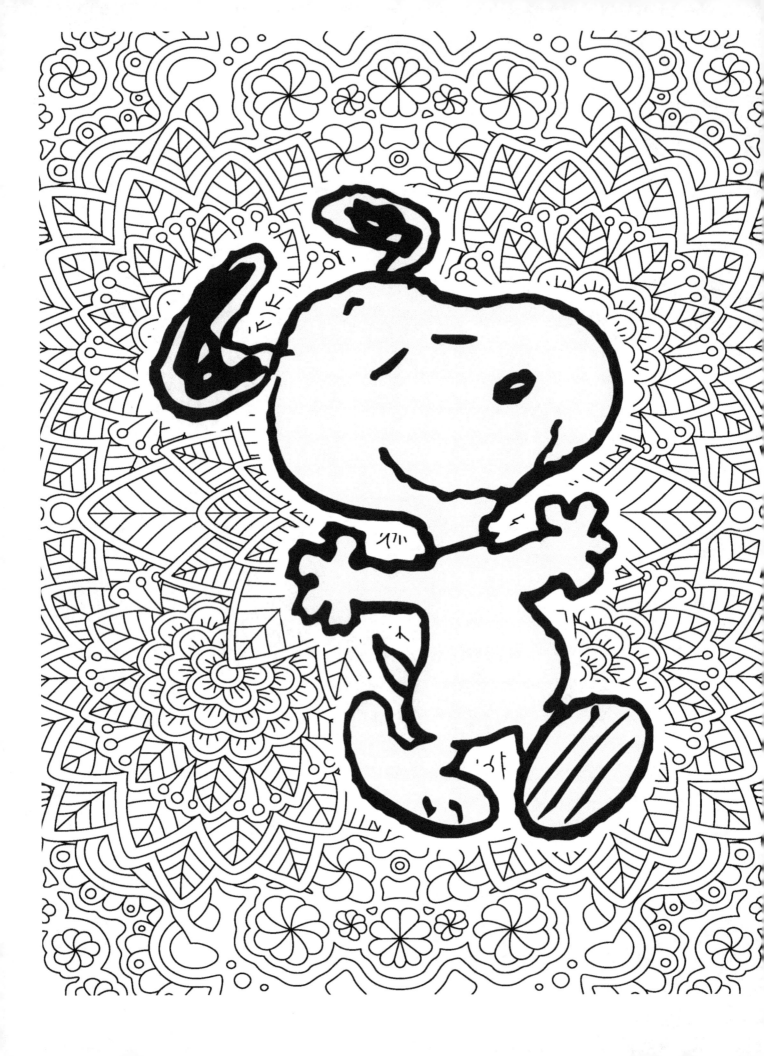

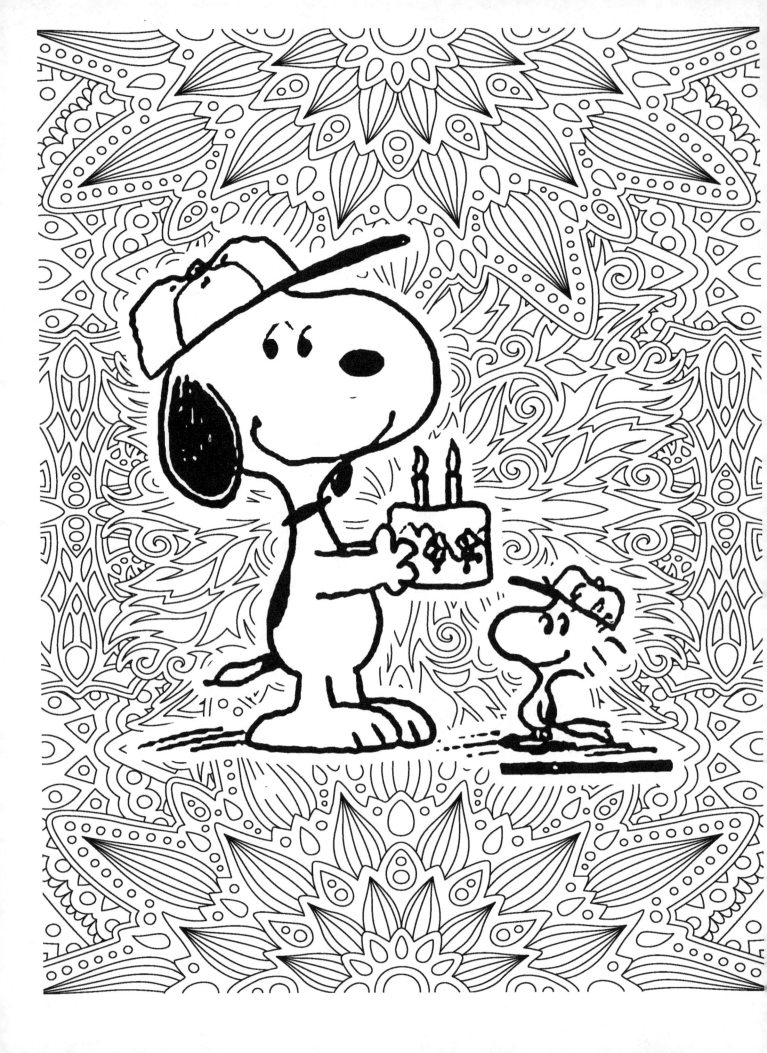

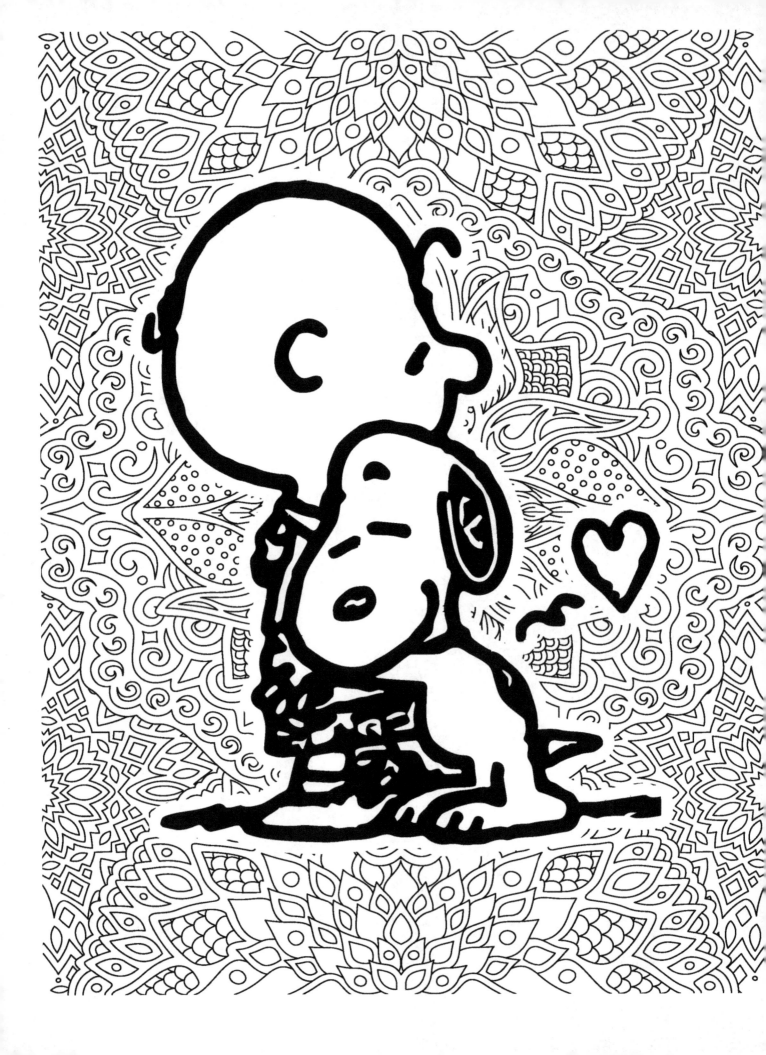

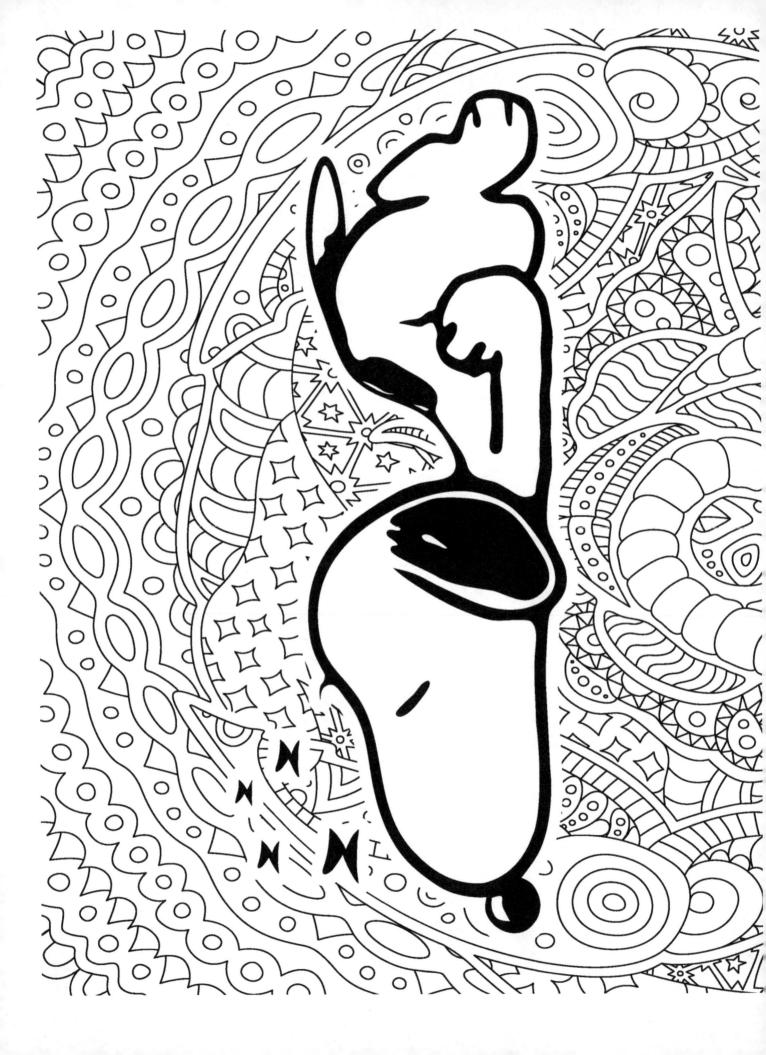

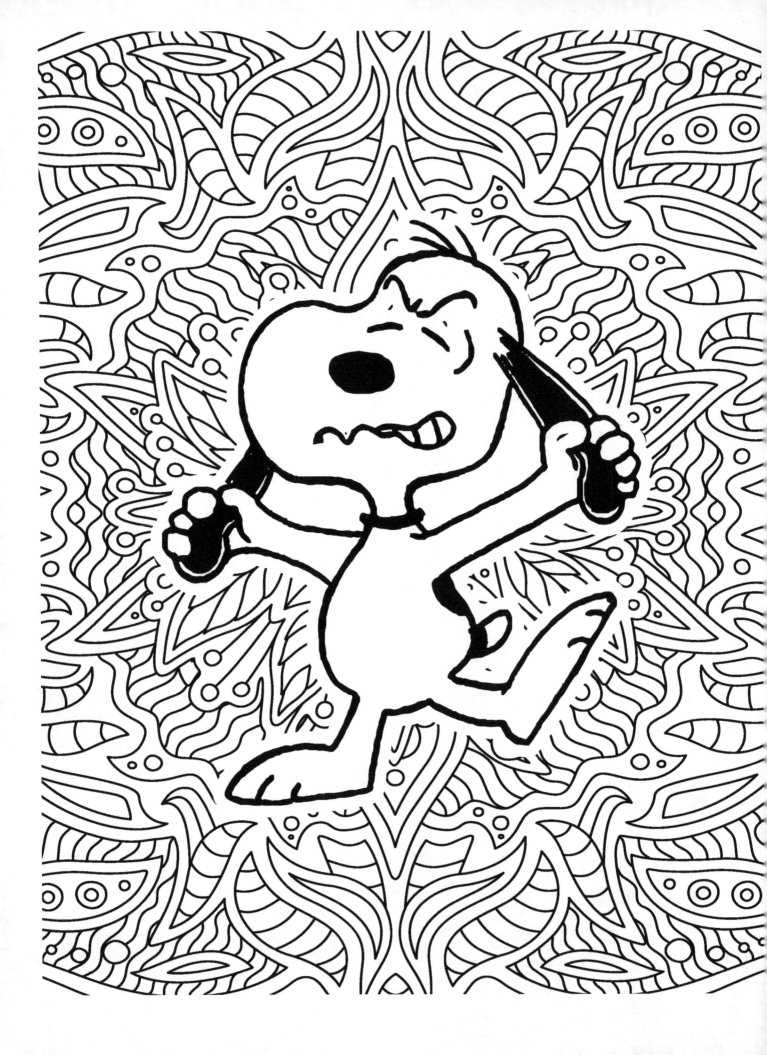

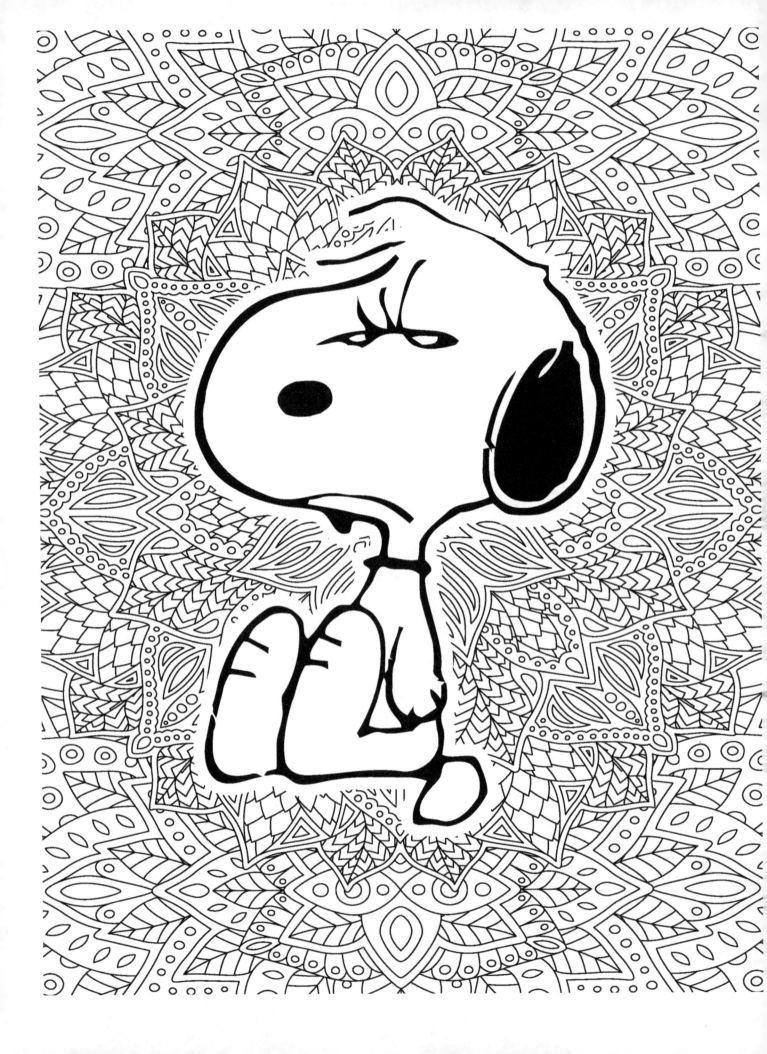

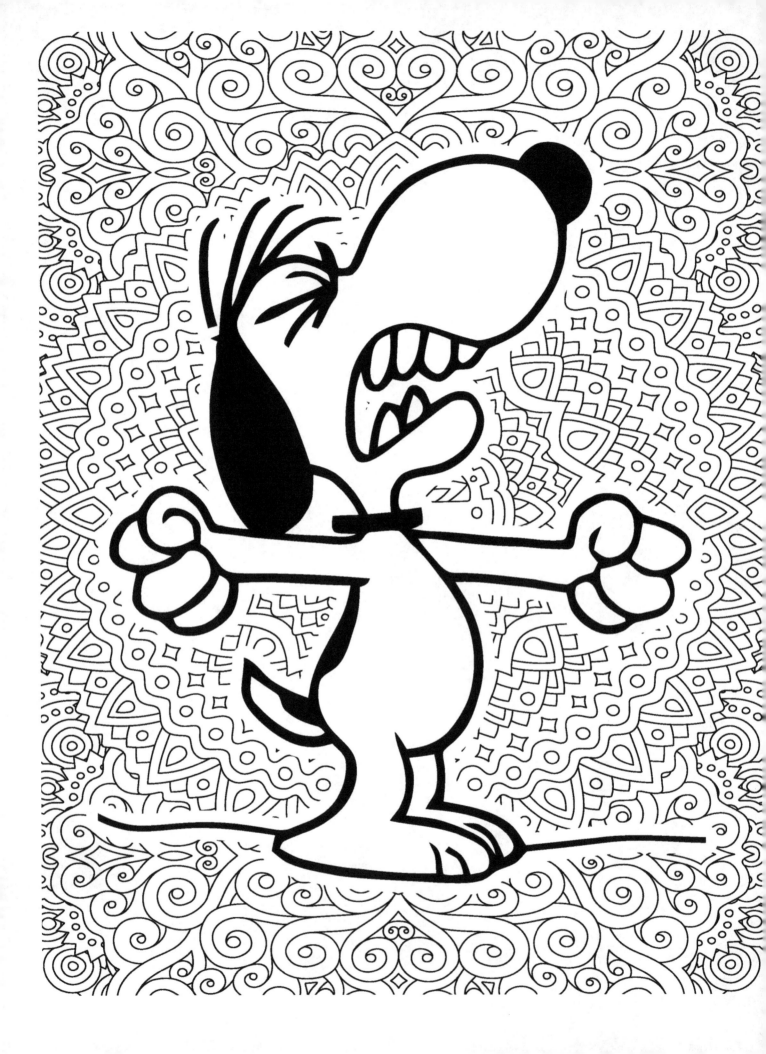

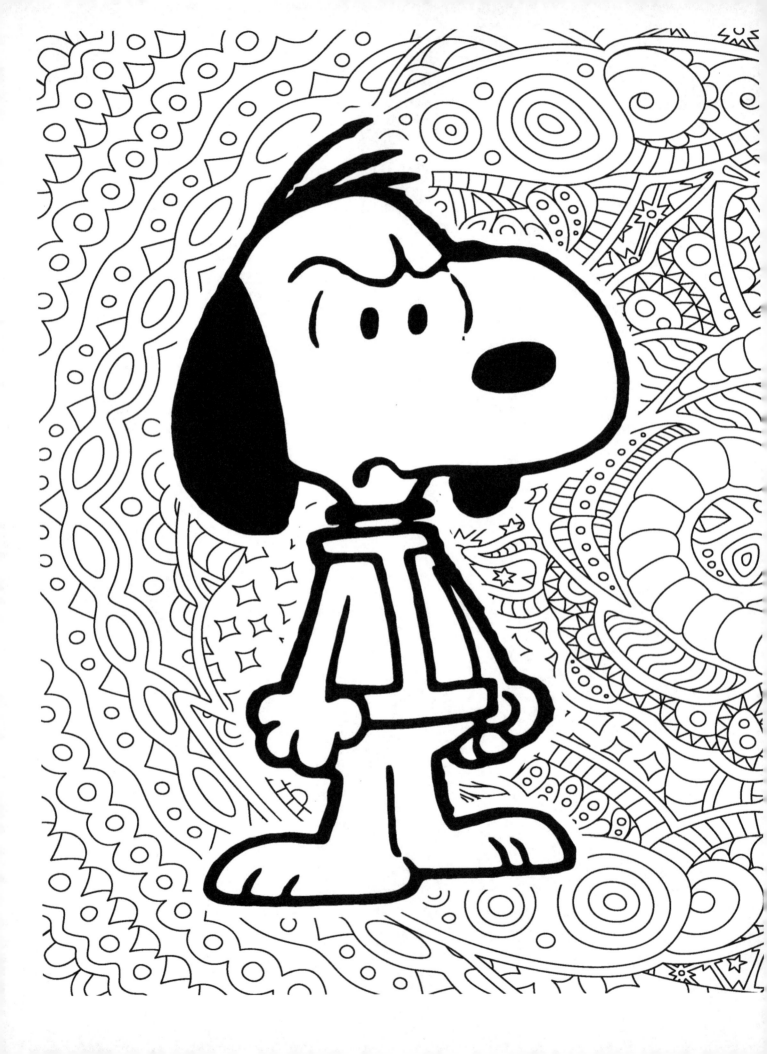

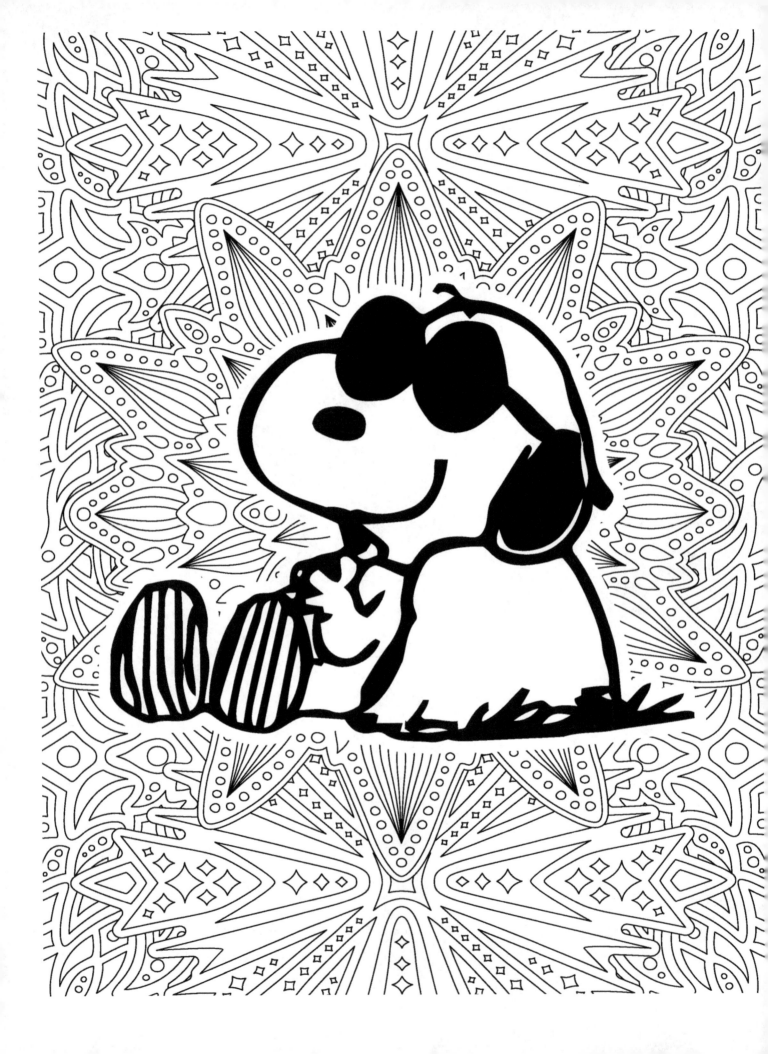

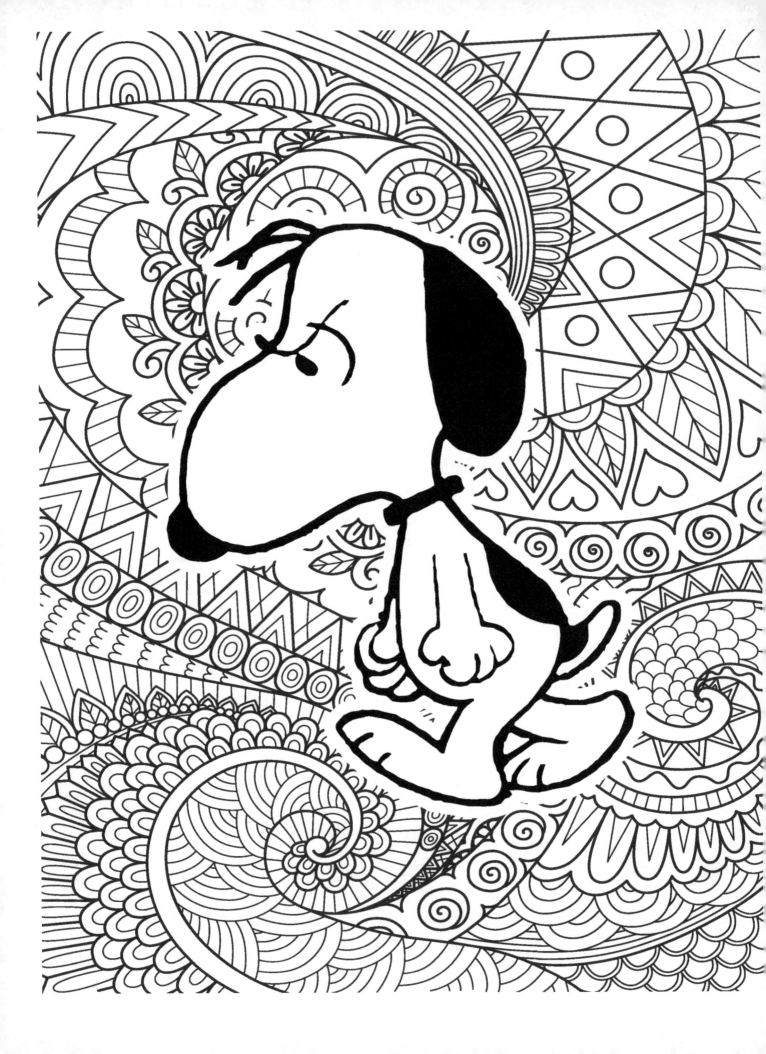

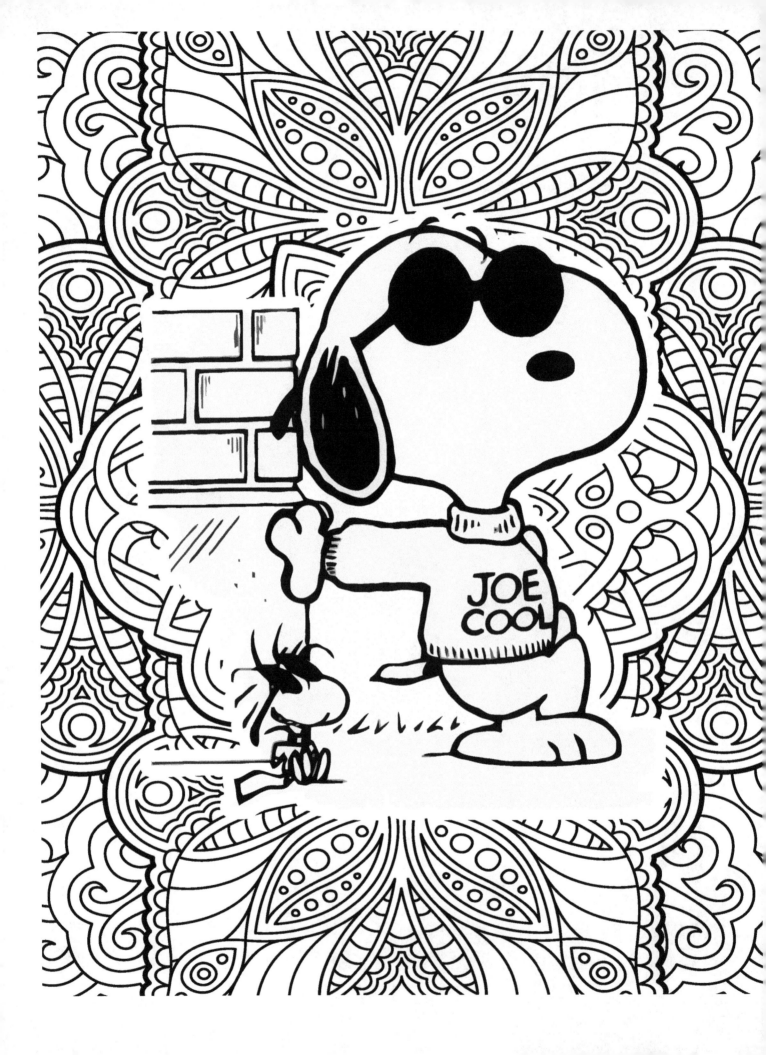

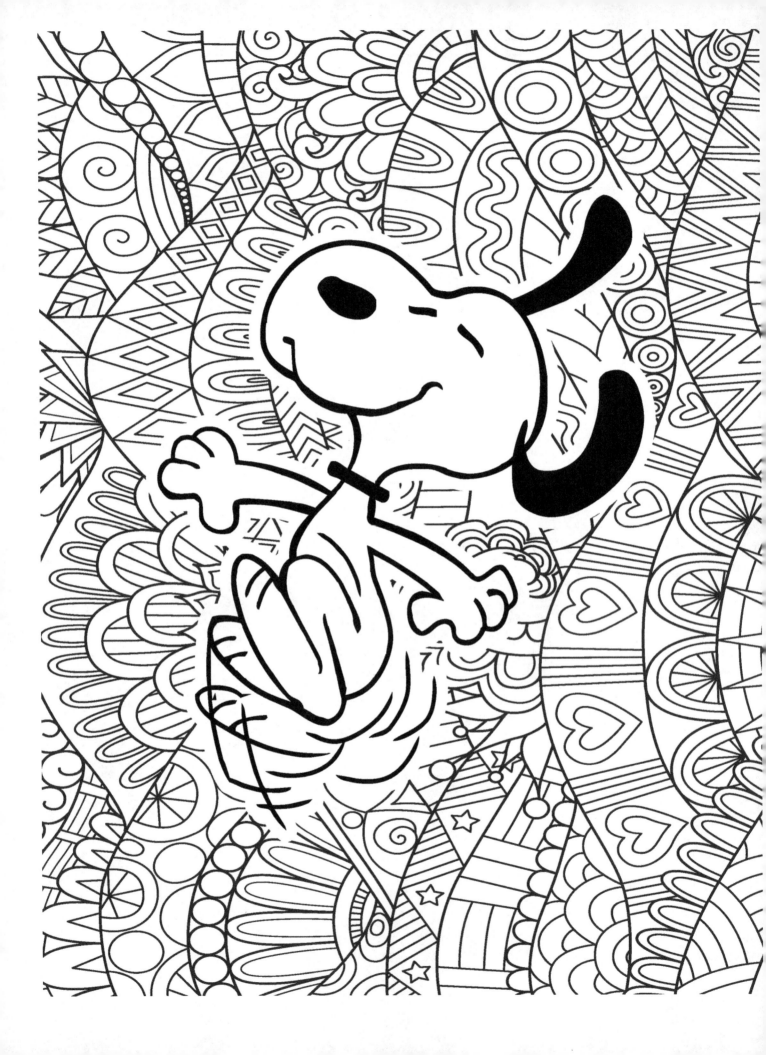

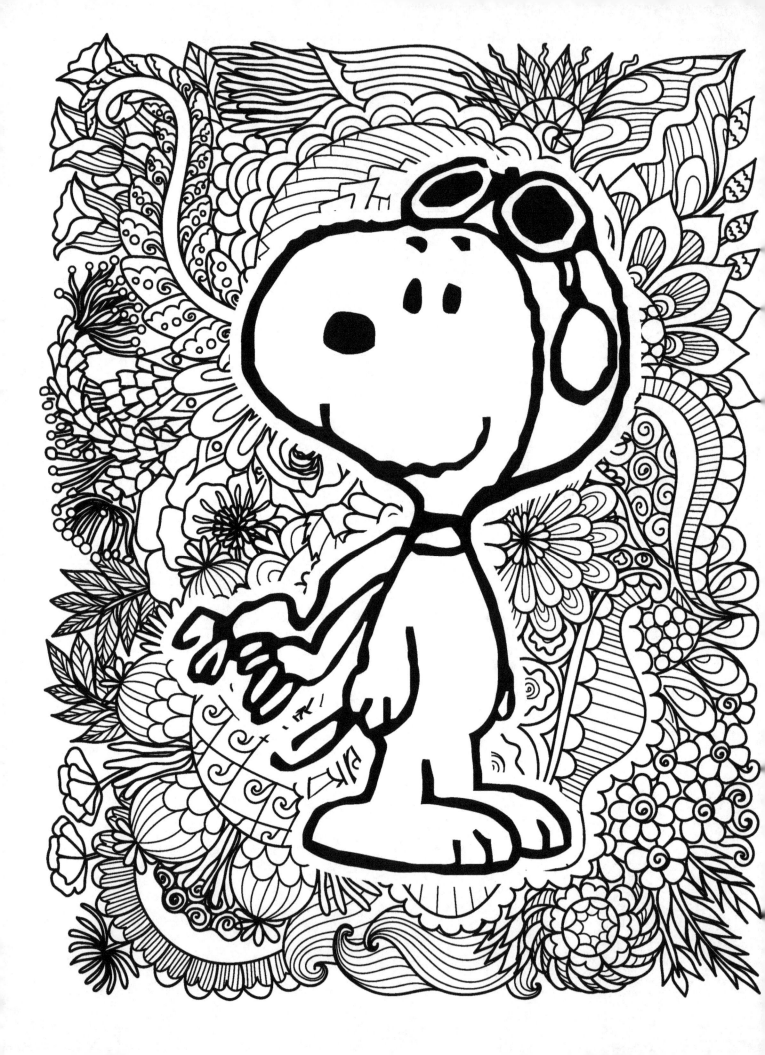

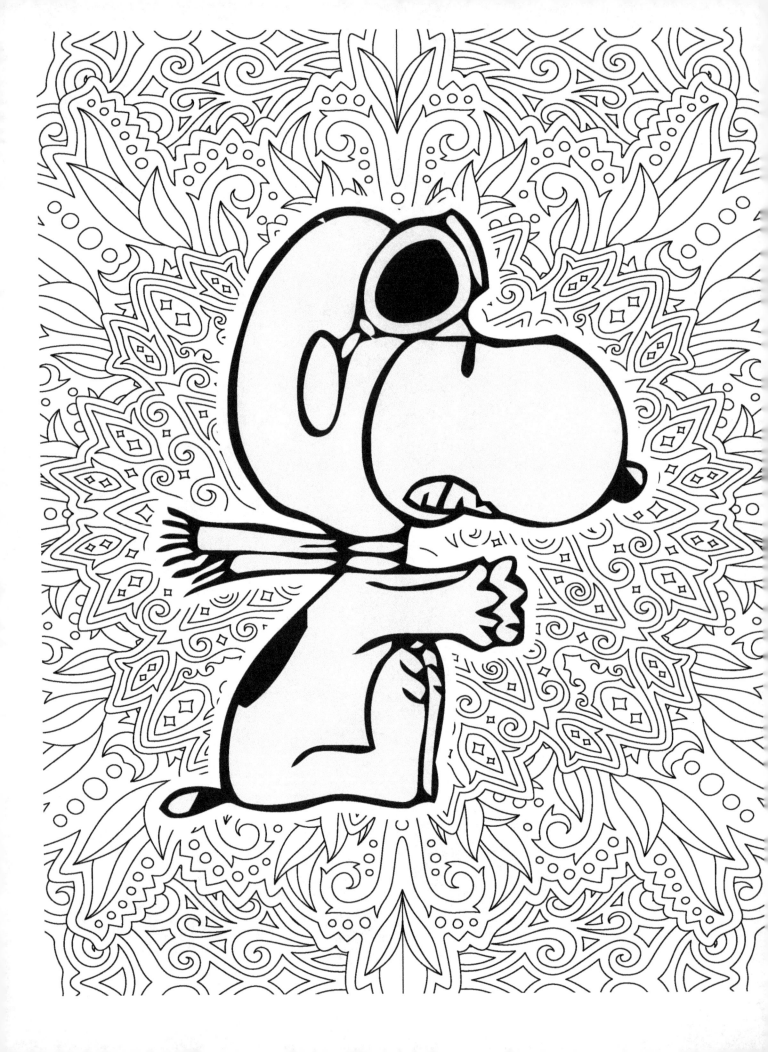

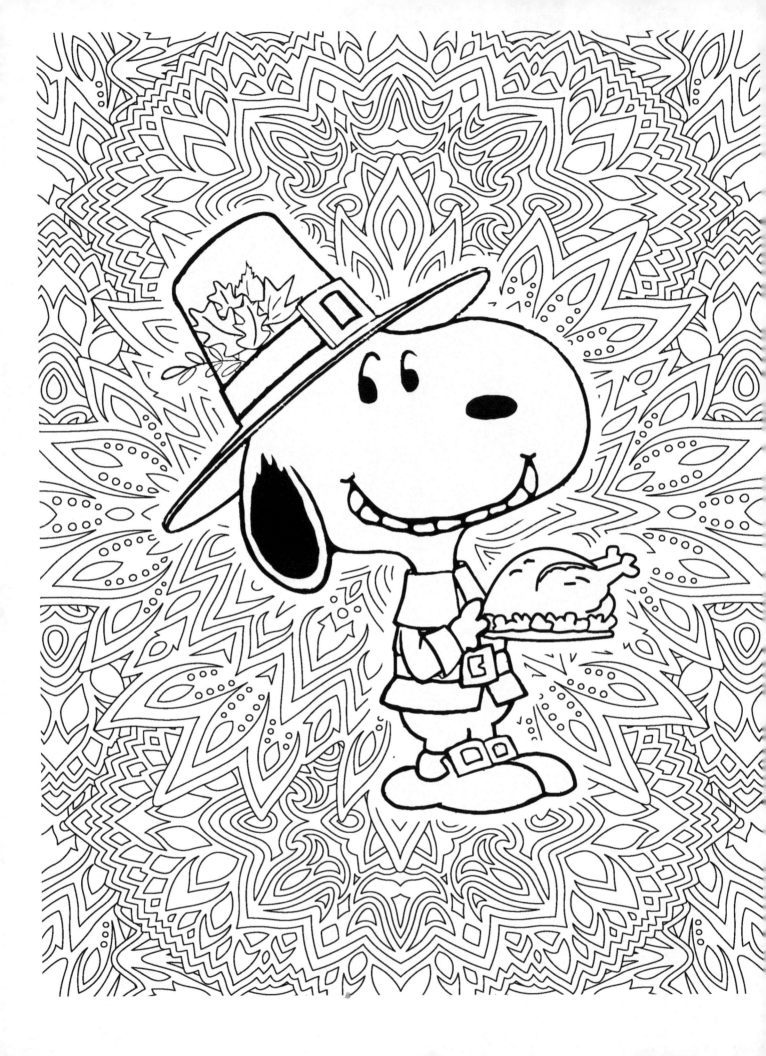

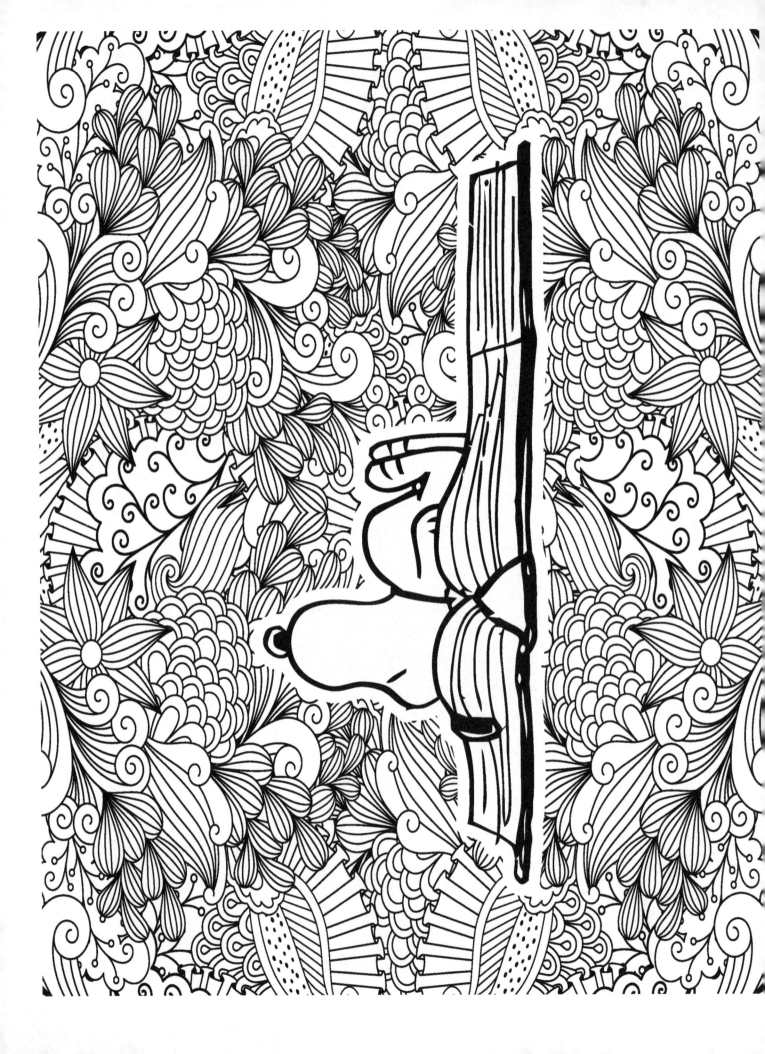

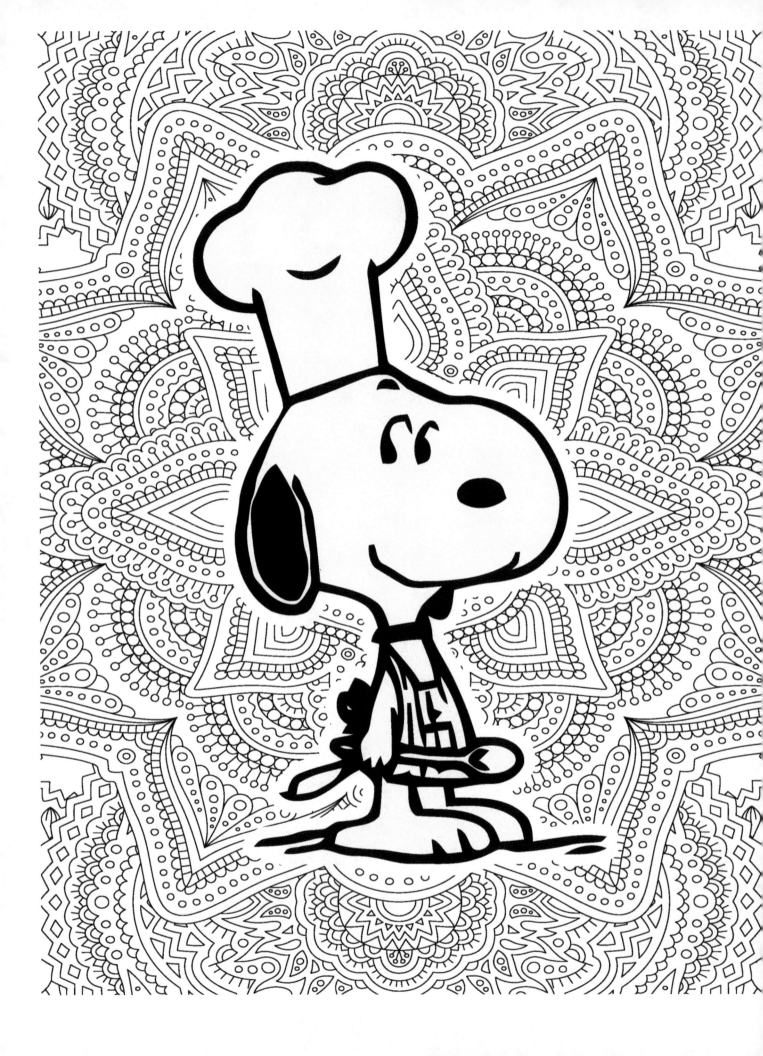

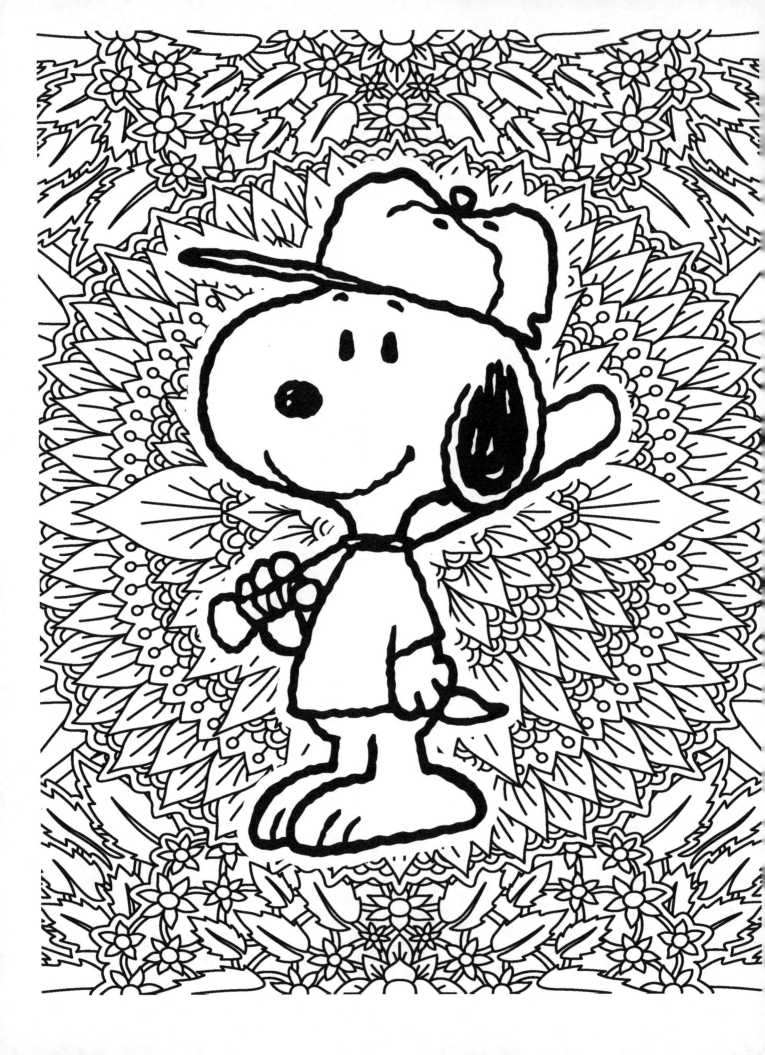

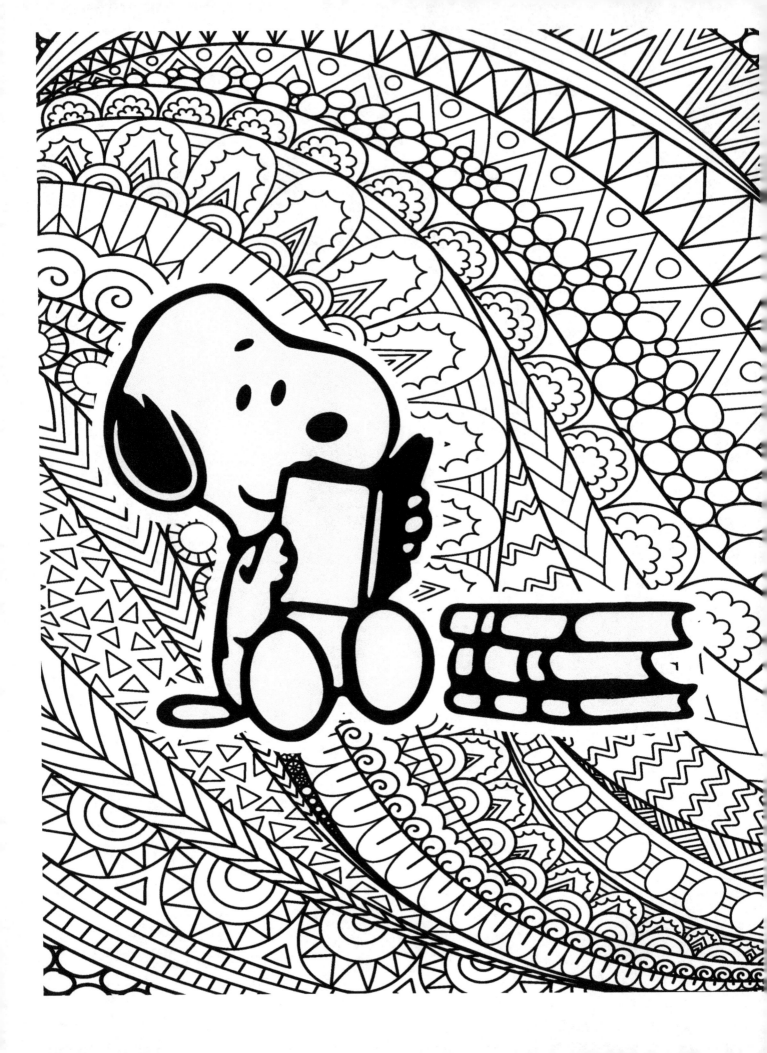

CPSIA information can be obtained
at www.ICGtesting.com
Printed in the USA
LVHW060315100921
697528LV00010B/139